D1224328

Edible Sunlight

Tara Haelle

Rourke
Educational Media

rourkeeducationalmedia.com

Before Reading:

Building Academic Vocabulary and Background Knowledge

Before reading a book, it is important to tap into what your child or students already know about the topic. This will help them develop their vocabulary, increase their reading comprehension, and make connections across the curriculum.

1. *Look at the cover of the book. What will this book be about?*
2. *What do you already know about the topic?*
3. *Let's study the Table of Contents. What will you learn about in the book's chapters?*
4. *What would you like to learn about this topic? Do you think you might learn about it from this book? Why or why not?*
5. *Use a reading journal to write about your knowledge of this topic. Record what you already know about the topic and what you hope to learn about the topic.*
6. *Read the book.*
7. *In your reading journal, record what you learned about the topic and your response to the book.*
8. *After reading the book complete the activities below.*

Content Area Vocabulary
Read the list. What do these words mean?

chlorophyl
decomposed
ecosystem
fertilization
iron
molecules
nitrogen
osmosis
phosphorus
photosynthesis
pollinate
predators
respiration
starch

After Reading:

Comprehension and Extension Activity

After reading the book, work on the following questions with your child or students in order to check their level of reading comprehension and content mastery.

1. *What is a fruit? How does it differ from a vegetable?* (Summarize)
2. *What are some reasons people should take steps to protect the environment?* (Infer)
3. *How do people benefit from photosynthesis?* (Asking questions)
4. *How might you use flowers to communicate with someone?* (Text to self connection)
5. *What would happen if the Amazon rainforest were destroyed?* (Asking questions)

Extension Activity

Create a slideshow or video explaining how photosynthesis works. Then demonstrate how both a hamburger and a salad can be considered edible sunlight.

Table of Contents

Energy from the Sun...4

Making Food 10

Parts of a Plant..16

Plant Reproduction 24

Cycles of Life...32

Plants and People 38

Glossary 46

Index...47

Show What You Know...47

Websites to Visit...47

About the Author...48

Energy from the Sun

Running, kicking a ball, singing, reading a book, sleeping … all these activities require energy. Your brain needs energy to think, your heart needs energy to beat, and your lungs need energy to breathe. In fact, all living organisms need energy for ten major processes.

10 Life Processes

Together, these processes are called an organism's metabolism.

Growth
life is always growing and developing

Absorption
transporting materials through membranes

Reproduction
creating more organisms of your own species

Digestion
grinding up and using food substances

Excretion
releasing wastes from the organism

Response to stimuli
responding to changes in the environment

Movement
even plants move!

Assimilation
building new materials from nutrients

Respiration
breathing

Circulation
distributing fluid, such as blood, throughout the body

Touch Me Not

Plants can move just like all other living creatures, but it's usually too slow for a person to see. Not so with the "touch-me-not" or "bashful" plant *Mimosa pudica*. When someone touches or shakes the leaves of this plant, it immediately folds up and droops. Scientists believe the plant is trying to protect itself from harm. After a few minutes, the leaves reopen.

People get that energy from food, including plants and animals. Animals get their food from other animals or from plants. Plants are the source of all other creatures' energy, but where do plants get their energy? They get it from food too, but they make it themselves. Think back to when you observed the sun's rays shining through a window or a cloud. Imagine if you could take a big bite out of those sunbeams. In a sense, you do that every time you eat. Plants make food using energy from the sun, and that same energy eventually makes its way to us in our food.

Growing Toward the Light

Plants must have light to make energy. If they are growing in a place with limited amounts of light, the plant will actually grow toward the light source. This phenomenon is called phototropism. You can watch it in action if you plant a seed in a pot and set it just out of reach of the window. The new plant will grow toward the window to get the light it needs.

It starts with the sun's rays. Those rays are actually waves of light and heat coming into the atmosphere. Energy that travels in waves is called radiant energy. The sun is Earth's main source of radiant energy. But people's bodies cannot use that energy in its raw form. Plants convert and store solar energy into atoms and link them together into **molecules**. These molecules contain stored energy. When molecules are mixed together, the chemical reactions that result release chemical energy the plant can use.

Because plants make food from the sun, they are called producers. Creatures that cannot make their own food are called consumers. Some consumers, such as cows or rabbits, eat only plants, which makes them primary consumers. They are also called herbivores, or plant eaters. Animals that eat other animals, such as a cheetah dining on a gazelle, are also consumers, but they are secondary consumers, called carnivores, or meat eaters. People are also consumers, but we are omnivores because we eat both plants and animals.

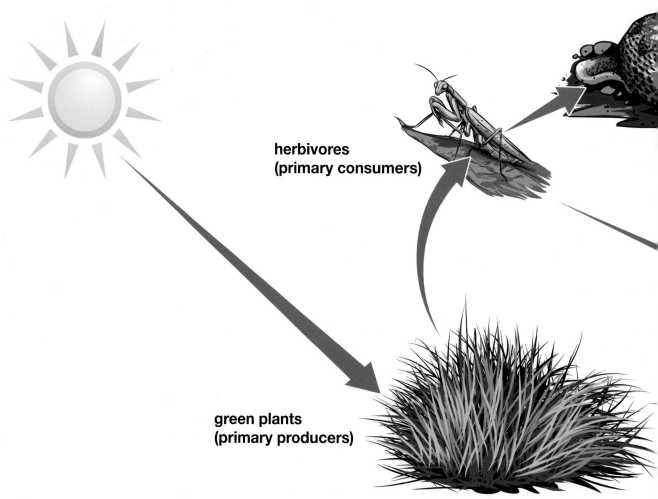

**herbivores
(primary consumers)**

**green plants
(primary producers)**

A third group called decomposers get energy from breaking down other living things, including all producers and consumers. Bacteria, certain worms, and fungi such as mushrooms are all decomposers. The nutrients that decomposers leave behind become important building blocks for producers in one of the many cycles of life.

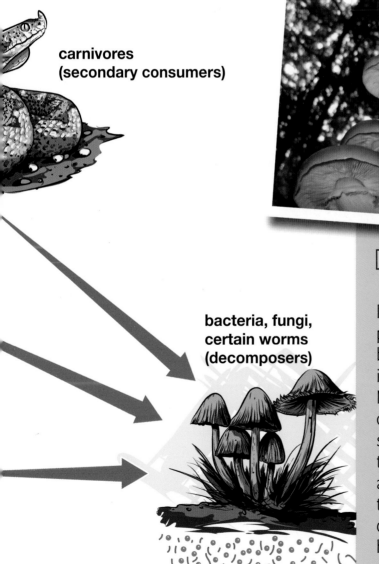

**carnivores
(secondary consumers)**

**bacteria, fungi,
certain worms
(decomposers)**

Humongous Fungus

What do you suppose is the largest living thing on Earth? Most people might guess the blue whale, but there's something bigger growing in the forests of Oregon's Blue Mountains. A type of honey fungus called *Armillaria ostoyae*, or "shoe-string" fungus, has been killing the trees of Malheur National Forest for at least 2,400 years—and it's all the same individual organism. The decomposer covers 2,385 acres (965 hectares) of the forest. That's equal to more than 1,800 football fields!

Making Food

The process of turning sunlight into food is called **photosynthesis**. The word *photo* means light, and the word *synthesis* means to combine chemical compounds together. Only plants that are green can carry out photosynthesis. That's because the substance that captures the sun's light in the plant is a green pigment called **chlorophyll**. Chlorophyll is stored in chloroplasts, an organized structure in plant cells. Chlorophyll gives plants their green color, and any green part of a plant has the ability to grab sunlight to start photosynthesis.

Carnivorous Plants

Even though plants make their own food, they need additional nutrients too. Some plants have developed a murderous mechanism for getting those nutrients if they don't get enough from the soil—they eat animals!

One of the best known of these plants is the Venus flytrap. At the tip of its leaves is a trap like an open clamshell. When beetles, spiders, grasshoppers, and other critters crawl across it, the trap snaps shut, and the plant digests the creature.

But other plants have other tricks up their leaves. Some trap insects or spiders with a sticky mucus or suck them into an internal airless space. Pitcher plants have pitfall traps—rolled leaves with a pool of digestion chemicals at the bottom. So far, though, no plants have been known to trap and digest humans. Whew!

Chloroplasts, visible here in the cells of the many-fruited thyme moss, are the energy factories filled with chlorophyll. A few bacteria also contain chlorophyll and can photosynthesize their food too.

Venus flytrap

pitcher plants

11

Photosynthesis

Chlorophyll is just one ingredient in the recipe for photosynthesis. Plants also need two other molecules to start the process, water (H_2O) and carbon dioxide (CO_2). The plant then combines water, carbon dioxide, and the sunlight's energy to create oxygen (O_2) and glucose, a type of sugar made from carbon, hydrogen, and oxygen ($C_6H_{12}O_6$). When six carbon dioxide molecules and six water molecules are mixed with sunlight, they produce six oxygen molecules and one molecule of glucose. Look at the chemical reaction equation below and count the hydrogen, carbon, and oxygen atoms on each side. You'll see they add up to six carbon atoms, 12 hydrogen atoms and 18 oxygen atoms on both sides.

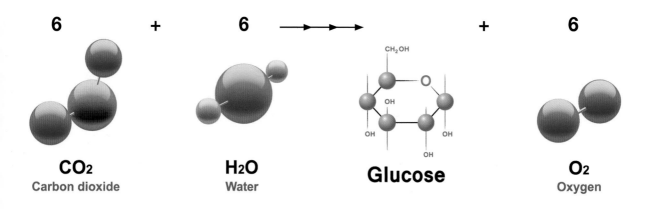

| 6 | + | 6 | $\longrightarrow$ | | + | 6 |

CO_2
Carbon dioxide

H_2O
Water

Glucose

O_2
Oxygen

Photosynthesis occurs into two sets of reactions. The first reaction requires light because it's the act of capturing sunlight and storing its energy in a chemical called ATP. The second reaction, called the "dark reaction," doesn't need light. The plant uses ATP to turn the carbon dioxide and water into glucose and oxygen. The plant doesn't need the oxygen and releases it as a waste product into the atmosphere.

The Calvin Cycle is the name of the second set of reactions in photosynthesis, when carbon dioxide is converted into sugar in the chloroplasts. It's named for Melvin Calvin, a California scientist who discovered it in 1957.

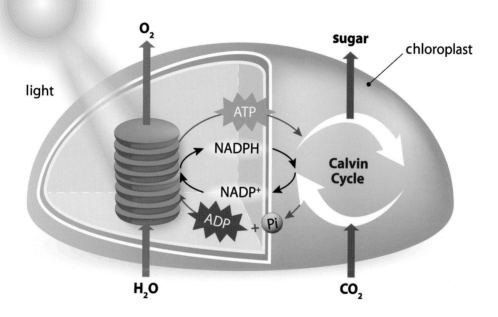

Grow Fresh Air

If communities of people ever end up living out in space, they will need clean air. Plants can help by constantly releasing oxygen, but they might do even more than that. NASA conducted a study to find out if certain plants could help remove pollutants from the air in a room. They focused on three chemicals that can be dangerous if people inhale too much of them: trichloroethylene, benzene, or formaldehyde. The plants they tested included the bamboo palm, Chinese evergreen, ficus, peace lily, English ivy, gerbera daisy, Janet Craig, marginata, mass cane, mother-in-law's tongue, pot mum, and warneckei. They found that every plant removed at least one of these chemicals in substantial amounts. So if you're looking for a green air filter system in your home, these plants might be a place to start.

Respiration

Just as one person's trash is another person's treasure, humans and other animals need the oxygen plants release as waste. Our bodies breathe in oxygen and combine it with sugar from our food to create energy in a process called cell **respiration**. The chemical reaction equation for respiration is very similar to photosynthesis in reverse:

$$C_6H_{12}O_6 + 6O_2 ===> 6CO_2 + 6H_2O + Energy$$

Notice that one of the products created during respiration is carbon dioxide. Our bodies don't need the carbon dioxide so we release it when we exhale along with some of the water vapor. These gases then re-enter the air where plants can use it for photosynthesis.

Lungs of the Earth

Take a deep breath. Of all those oxygen molecules you inhaled, about one in every five exists thanks to the Amazon rainforest. The Amazon covers more than a billion acres (404,685,642 hectares) across five South American countries, and it's dense with trees, flowers, bushes, and other plants taking in carbon dioxide and releasing oxygen. Some people have nicknamed the Amazon the "lungs of the planet" because it produces about 20 percent of the world's oxygen.

Starch Storage

As busy food factories, plants constantly need to use the energy they create from sunlight, so their cells carry out respiration as well. Day and night, they are converting glucose into energy even as they are manufacturing more glucose. But they don't use all the glucose they make right away. They store it as back-up fuel in case they go days or weeks without sunlight.

Glucose doesn't store very well on its own, though. It's a small molecule that can escape the cell or dissolve in water, and it would get crowded in a cell with strings and strings of glucose floating around. So plants convert glucose into **starch** to store it in plant cells. Starch is a type of carbohydrate, a train of small sugars linked together like boxcars. Starch doesn't dissolve in water and is too big to seep out of plants, but it's compact enough to get out of the way of other cell parts doing their jobs. Whenever the plant needs more glucose, it converts the starch back into individual glucose molecules.

Many vegetables people eat are high in starch, such as peas, corn, chestnuts, and potatoes.

Parts of a Plant

Chloroplasts store chlorophyll and carry out photosynthesis, but chloroplasts aren't hanging out in plant cells all by themselves. They are one of many different organelles. Organelles, like organs in a body, are organized structures in the cell that carry out specific functions. The cell holds them together with a cell membrane, which is enclosed by an outer cell wall. The diagram shows the major parts of a plant cell.

Plant Cell

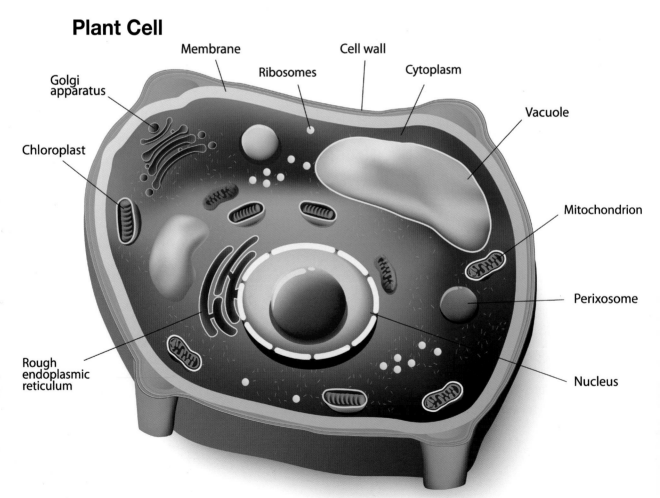

Membrane

Ribosomes

Cell wall

Cytoplasm

Golgi apparatus

Vacuole

Chloroplast

Mitochondrion

Perixosome

Rough endoplasmic reticulum

Nucleus

Plant Cells

The cell wall is a thick, rigid membrane made of a substance called cellulose. The cell wall provides the cell itself with support but also binds with other cells' walls to give the plant a sturdy structure. Within the wall is the thinner cell membrane, the cell's gatekeeper. The cell membrane is a layer of protein and fat that lets some materials in and out while preventing others from passing through.

Within the cell itself is the cytoplasm, the jellylike substance that holds all the organelles and the cell nucleus. The nucleus is the brain of the cell. It uses proteins to direct the cell's functions, and it contains

The way cytoplasm holds together organelles resembles the way a gelatin salad holds fruits together.

the DNA, the genetic instructions for all life.

Other major organelles include mitochondria, ribosomes, and Golgi bodies. Mitochondria are like tiny batteries that convert the energy from glucose into ATP to use during photosynthesis and respiration. Ribosomes are protein factories that build proteins using instructions from RNA, another type of genetic material. The Golgi body is a packaging center for proteins and carbohydrates the cell needs to export. The Golgi body bundles them together into sacs called vesicles that can pass through the cell membrane.

Standing Firm

Plant cells also contain a large space called a vacuole that's filled with water. Vacuoles take up most of the space in a cell and serve several functions. One of their main functions is keeping the cell's shape. When a plant has sufficient water, the vacuole fills up with water. The cell becomes swollen and hard, which scientists describe as turgid. In a plant with too little water, the vacuole drains, and the plant cell becomes flaccid. Together, flaccid plant cells cause leaves and flower petals to wilt and a stem to droop. Vacuoles are therefore essential for a plant to remain firm and upright so that it can continue to absorb sunlight.

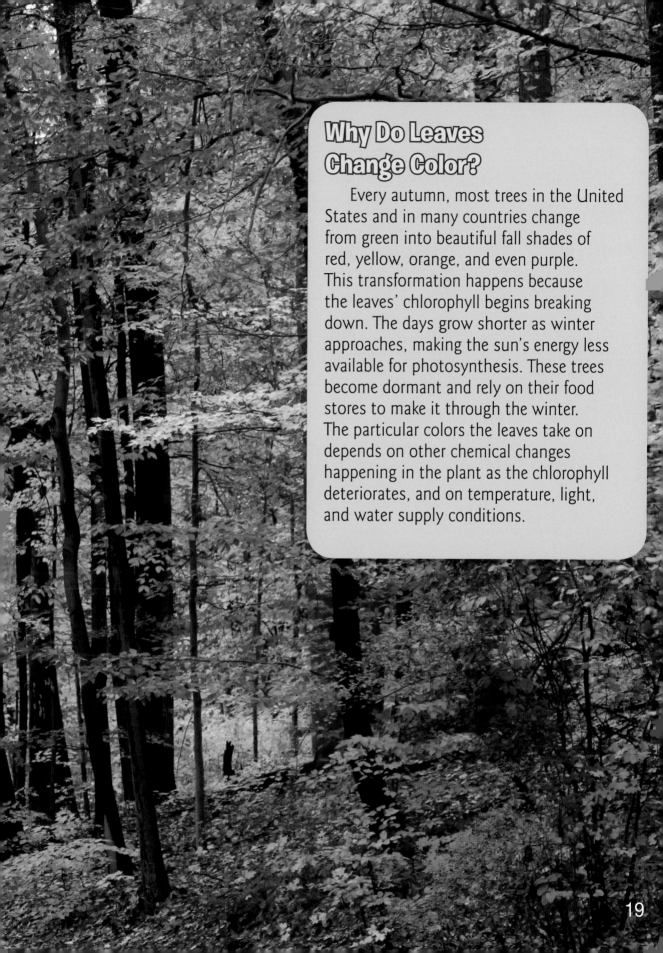

Why Do Leaves Change Color?

Every autumn, most trees in the United States and in many countries change from green into beautiful fall shades of red, yellow, orange, and even purple. This transformation happens because the leaves' chlorophyll begins breaking down. The days grow shorter as winter approaches, making the sun's energy less available for photosynthesis. These trees become dormant and rely on their food stores to make it through the winter. The particular colors the leaves take on depends on other chemical changes happening in the plant as the chlorophyll deteriorates, and on temperature, light, and water supply conditions.

Leaves, Roots, and Stems

Plants share several basic structures. Roots at the bottom of a plant anchor it in place, take up nutrients from the soil, and store extra food for the plant. They also absorb water from the ground through a process called **osmosis**. When a highly concentrated solution sits beside a less concentrated one, water will move from the lower concentration to the higher one until the concentrations are equal. This process of osmosis draws water in through the cell membranes of plant cells.

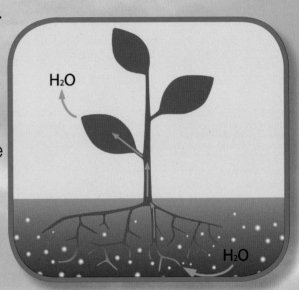

H_2O

H_2O

Camels of the Plant World

A plant's roots can store food when times get tough, but for plants growing in the desert, that usually isn't enough. In such a dry environment with little rainfall, they need to store water for those tough times too. Many desert plants, such as species of cactus, have thick stems or leaves that store water.

They have also developed ways to hang on to every last drop as long as possible. The thick, waxy skin on a cactus prevents the water from escaping easily, and its prickly spines stop animals from trying to steal a sip. Another trick is opening up their stomata at night instead of the day to reduce how much water they might lose to evaporation. All these adaptations help cacti survive the harshest conditions of the dry desert.

Osmosis in Action

You can observe osmosis in your own home. You'll need the following materials:

- a glass of water
- your favorite color food coloring
- either a celery stalk or fresh white flower

Instructions:

1. Put a drop of food coloring into the glass of water.
2. Place the celery stalk or flower stem in it.
3. Leave it overnight.
4. The next day, look at the bottom of the celery or flower stem. What do you see?

Over time, the colored water will travel all the way to the top. If you used blue water, you'll soon have a blue flower instead of a white one!

Much like the roots, stems provide support to plants too, but they also house the superhighway system for distributing water, nutrients, and food throughout a plant. Two major components in the stem are the xylem and the phloem, which make up the plant's circulatory system. If you think of these as two lanes on the superhighway, xylem is the water lane, and phloem is the food lane. Xylem cells transport water and nutrients from the roots, and phloem cells transport food made in the leaves.

Cross-section of a Stem

phloem tube

xylem tube

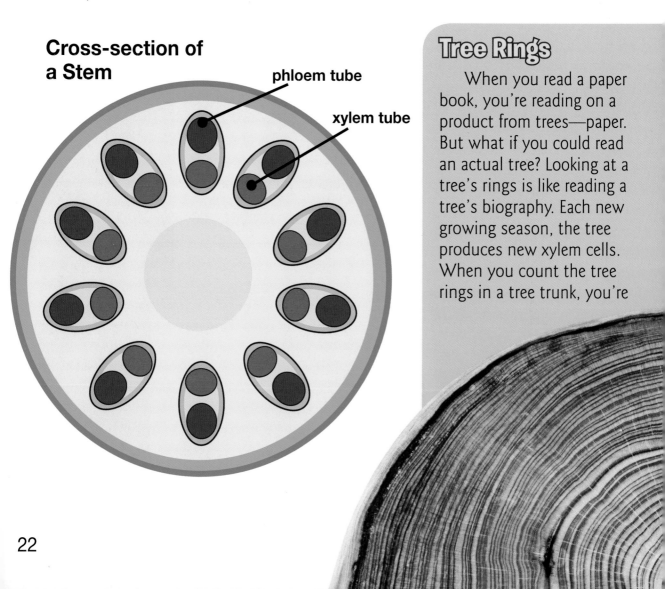

Tree Rings

When you read a paper book, you're reading on a product from trees—paper. But what if you could read an actual tree? Looking at a tree's rings is like reading a tree's biography. Each new growing season, the tree produces new xylem cells. When you count the tree rings in a tree trunk, you're

Leaves are the factory floor for photosynthesis. They tend to be thin and flat because their main purpose is to capture sunlight and conduct photosynthesis. Being wide, thin, and flat gives them as much surface area as possible to absorb sunlight. Leaves also contain very tiny pores called stomata that open up to capture carbon dioxide and also let plants "sweat." Each pore is called a stoma. Water escapes from the stomata and then evaporates.

counting the rings of xylem tissue. People can learn a lot about a tree's history through these rings. The thicker the ring, the better a growing season that year was. In years of drought, rings will be very narrow. You can also see evidence of floods, lightning strikes or fires, earthquakes, or insect infestations in a tree's rings.

Leaves are thin enough for light to pass through them, ensuring that every cell's chloroplasts can capture some light.

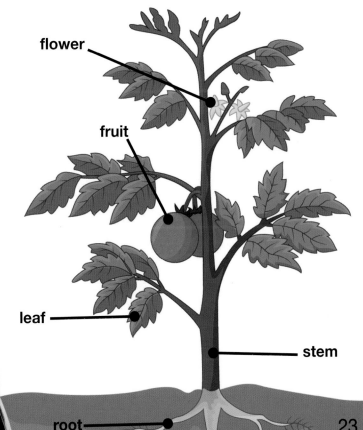

flower

fruit

leaf

stem

root

Plant Reproduction

The flowers, fruit, and seeds of plants make up its reproductive system. All organisms must reproduce to continue survival, and many plants actually rely on other creatures, especially insects, to help them in sexual reproduction. Sexual reproduction involves the contribution of different cells from two different organisms, each containing half the DNA needed for the new life. One cell comes from a male, and one cell comes from a female. **Fertilization** is the process of the two different cells joining together.

Sexual Parts of a Flower

The male and female parts of a plant are contained within its flowers. The blooming of a flower indicates that a flower is ready for sexual reproduction. The female part of the flower is called the pistil, a long, thin structure in the middle of flower, made up of the style, stigma, and ovary. The style is the stalk itself, and the sticky bulb at the top is the stigma. The ovary at the base of the style contains ovules that become seeds. Flowers have multiple male parts called stamens, each made of a filament and an anther. The anther is the pouch of pollen at the top of the filament, a stalk about as thin as a strand of hair.

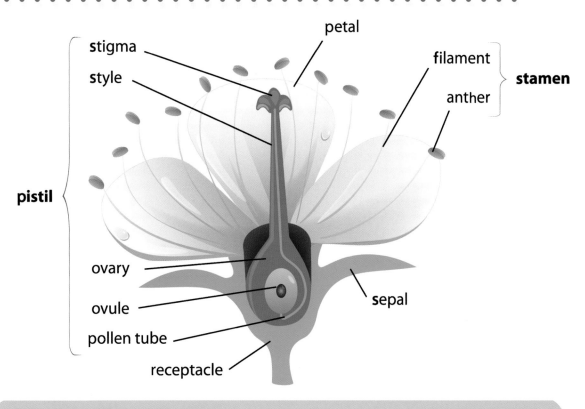

petal

stigma

style

filament

stamen

anther

pistil

ovary

ovule

pollen tube

sepal

receptacle

The 100-Year Flower

Imagine if it took you 100 years to reach puberty. For a flower that grows in the Andes Mountains of South America, that's just life. The flower's scientific name is *Puya raimondii*, but many call it the "Queen of the Andes," or the 100-year flower because it takes a century to bloom. It's also the largest plant in the Andes, growing to more than 30 feet (9 meters) high. When these desert plants bloom, about 30,000 white flowers sprout from the top of a central stalk, but this is the plant's last hurrah. Shortly afterward, the plant dies.

These conifers use the wind to spread their pollen. This method of pollination works best among tall trees in open areas where they can take advantage of the wind.

Pollination

For fertilization to occur, pollen must reach the sticky stigma and travel down the style to the ovary where it meets with the ovules. Then the ovary enlarges into a fruit as the seeds ripen. The process of the pollen getting to the pistil is pollination. Pollination occurs in different ways depending on the plant. For some plants, the wind is enough to carry pollen from one to another, especially if the stamens and pistils are long or stick out far from the flower.

For many plants, though, animals and insects play a huge role in pollination. The colorful petals of a flower attract bees, hummingbirds, butterflies, and other creatures who feed on pollen or the sweet nectar at the bottom of flowers. The strong scent of a flower also attracts these pollinators. Fortunately for the plant, these creatures tend to be messy eaters, getting pollen all over themselves during their meal. When they head off to another flower for their next course, the pollen rubs off on the new flower's stigma, beginning the process of fertilization.

pollen

Bee Colony Collapses

One of the most important pollinators on Earth is the honeybee. They aren't called busy bees for nothing! Farmers rely on bees to **pollinate** their crops, sometimes hiring local beekeepers when not enough wild bees come to visit. Some of our most familiar staple foods require bees. Apples and avocados, cashews and cucumbers, carrots and coffee, broccoli and beets, lemons and limes, pumpkins and peaches, strawberries and blueberries, walnuts and watermelons— these are a tiny few of the long list of foods needing bees.

But a disturbing trend has been occurring across the world in recent years. Bee colonies— massive communities of bees living together—have been collapsing. The bees head off for the day's work, but then they don't come home. Almost one third of U.S. honeybee colonies have disappeared. Even worse, scientists don't entirely understand why. They have some ideas, but many are studying the problem in hopes of stopping it.

Seed Dispersal

Once the seeds have matured, they need to leave their parent and find a place to grow into a new plant. The way seeds spread out is called seed dispersal. Seeds can disperse on their own, through the wind, by water, or with the help of animals, including humans.

Some seeds don't need any help. They fall to the ground and roll off, or they're contained within seed pods that dry and burst open, scattering the seeds inside. Other seeds ride the wind, such as those of dandelions. Each time you blow the soft puff of a dandelion flower, you're helping all those seeds find a new home to grow. Seeds of plants near or in water float off to new areas. Rainwater can also carry seeds far from their flowers.

The seeds of maple trees are commonly called helicopters because of the way they spin and drift toward the ground when released from the tree.

Seed Banks

The world can be a harsh place, especially with the climate changing over the years. Plants that cannot adapt or that become endangered run the risk of becoming extinct. That's why people are trying to preserve seeds from as many plants on Earth as possible. Whether they are collecting the seeds of crops we eat or those of species on the verge of disappearing, people are storing the seeds in seed banks throughout the world. Like high security banks that keep your money secure, seed banks maintain the right conditions for keeping the seeds safe. An estimated 1,000 seed banks exist around the world, maintained by nonprofit organizations, governments, and private organizations.

It might sound gross, but hitching a ride through an animal's digestive system is a double bonus for seeds. They get carried far from their parent plant and are surrounded by rich nutrients when released in excrement, or poop.

In their race to hoard as many acorns as possible, squirrels are basically little gardeners. They forget where they bury most of the acorns, so they basically plant dozens of baby oak trees.

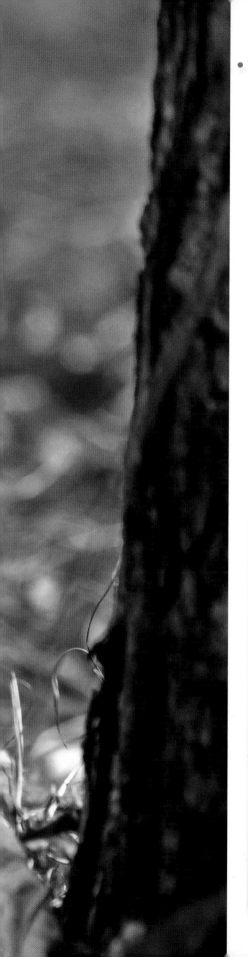

Animals transport seeds several different ways. Birds, mammals, reptiles, and other creatures that eat fruit often do not digest the seeds. They release the seeds back into the world through their waste. Seeds with barbs or hooks may hitch a ride on an animal's fur—or a person's pant leg—to travel to a new place. Other seeds are physically carried by animals, such as acorns gathered and buried by squirrels. The acorns the squirrels forget about may grow into a new oak tree.

Fruit or Vegetable?

You say a tomato is a fruit, and your friend says a tomato is a vegetable. Who's right? Cut open a tomato and look. Are there seeds? If so, it's a fruit. A fruit is the ripened ovaries of a plant. So even though we think of cucumbers, pumpkins, squash, and string beans as vegetables, they are actually different types of fruit.

Cycles of Life

The cycle of producers, consumers, and decomposers is just one of many cycles that dominate all aspects of our world. Nearly everything on Earth runs in cycles because the planet has a limited supply of resources. Very little is going out or coming in from outer space except the sun's light and heat. In fact, you could think of the Earth as a giant machine powered by the sun's energy with many smaller gears always turning.

Several of those gears include the most important building blocks for life: the elements oxygen, carbon, hydrogen, and **nitrogen**. Each of these elements follow their own cycles. The complementary processes of photosynthesis and respiration show how oxygen, carbon, and hydrogen cycle through life, Earth, and the atmosphere. Nitrogen follows a similar path.

The atmosphere is like an outer shell to the energy machine of Earth. Oxygen makes up about a fifth of the atmosphere, and nearly all the rest is nitrogen. Other gases make up less than one percent of the atmosphere.

Rotating Crops

Everybody needs a break now and then—even the soil. When plants grow from the ground, they use nutrients they pull from the earth. Farmers growing crops on the same land over and over will eventually use up all the nutrients there. They can use fertilizers to replace most of these nutrients, but they can also just give the land a rest. By leaving a field fallow for a period of time and rotating their crops among different fields, the farmer gives the ground a chance to recover and become rich again with necessary nutrients.

Water Cycle

Another important cycle on Earth is the water cycle, also called the hydrologic cycle. The sun's energy causes the surface water of ponds, lakes, rivers, and oceans to evaporate, turning from liquid into a gas. The water vapor then rises into the atmosphere and begins to cool. As it cools, the water molecules grow closer and closer together and form clouds. Soon, they cool enough to turn back into a liquid, a process called condensation. When the clouds become too heavy with water, the water falls back to the Earth as rain, snow, sleet, or hail. It becomes runoff and heads back to rivers, lakes, and oceans, continuing the cycle.

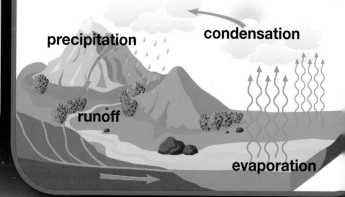

Nitrogen Cycle

Although you can't see it, nitrogen makes up the majority of our atmosphere, the layer of air that encircles the Earth. All living creatures need nitrogen, but most cannot grab it out of the air to use any more than humans can take actual bites out of sunbeams. Only some bacteria and algae can take nitrogen from the air and turn it into nitrates, the form found in soil that other creatures can use. Plants take up nitrates through their roots, then link them with carbon atoms to create amino acids, enzymes, or nucleic acids. Amino acids make up proteins, and nucleic acids make up DNA. Enzymes are substances that cause necessary chemical reactions in the body, such as breaking down food during digestion.

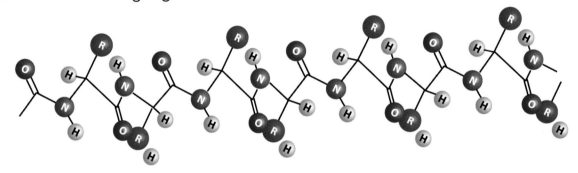

Proteins are like a long chain where each link is a different amino acid.

Consumers get the nitrogen they need by eating plants and other consumers. Nitrates then return to the soil in two ways, poop and death. Animals excrete nitrates in their waste, and after creatures die, decomposers break down organisms into their components, including nitrates. The cycle continues.

Iron

Another key element for living organisms is **iron**, found in the soil, in rocks, and in the dust of volcanic eruptions. Many enzymes require iron, and iron helps humans' red blood cells carry oxygen throughout our body. Like other elements, iron is exchanged between plants and animals in a cycle.

red blood cells

Phosphorous

Phosphorus is another vital element plants use in the form of phosphates. Most phosphorus is in rocks, which the rain wears down and carries into the soil. Plants pull phosphates from the soil, and consumers get them through food. But phosphorus is gradually leaving its cycle when phosphates make their way to the ocean and sink. They are carried by water runoff or animal waste. Plants and animals cannot use the phosphates on the sea floor, but people need them to grow crops after the previous crop has used them up from the soil. People must artificially replace phosphates with fertilizers, such as manure, to grow more crops.

35

Become a Leaf Detective

The most important nutrients all plants need are called macronutrients. These include nitrogen, potassium, sulfur, calcium, magnesium, and phosphorus. When a plant doesn't have enough of one of these, it affects the way its leaves look. Some of these changes can overlap, especially if the plant has more than one deficiency, but you can learn to recognize what nutrients a plant is missing by inspecting its leaves.

Materials: All you need is this book and a nearby place with plants. You could take a walk around the neighborhood checking out your neighbors' gardens, walk around a local park or your school grounds, or visit a botanical garden. You could also bring a camera to photograph the plants' leaves and then analyze the photos at home with this book.

How the leaf looks		Missing nutrient
New leaves at the top of the plant become irregularly shaped. If the plant has visible fruit, it may look rotted or black where the fruit's blossom grew.		calcium
Older leaves at the bottom of the plant are yellow, and the other leaves are light green or yellowing.		nitrogen
Only the edges of leaves turn yellow while the inner part of the leaves look arrowhead-shaped.		magnesium
Older leaves at the bottom of the plant have turned very dark green or reddish purple, and the tips of other leaves look burnt.		phosphorous
The edges of leaves, especially older ones, look brownish or blackish like they've been burnt. The leaves wilt or fold inward.		potassium

Food Webs

As matter and energy travel through cycles on Earth, they use living organisms as vessels. Energy travels up the food chain from grass to zebra to lion or from algae to minnow to barracuda to shark. At the end of each food chain are the top, or apex, **predators**, the secondary consumers who do not have any other predators to watch out for. Only after death will decomposers feed on them.

But food chains overlap and intersect with one another. The same bird that eats flies and spiders might also eat the frogs feeding on those same flies and spiders. Intersecting food chains that depend on one another are called food webs. The interconnectedness of food webs make up an **ecosystem**, the entire community of living organisms in a particular environment. Much like a game of Jenga, removing just one piece of the ecosystem has the potential to bring the rest of it crashing down.

Plants and People

It might be easy to forget that plants are all around us sometimes, but we would certainly notice if they vanished. In fact, we wouldn't be able to survive. People depend on plants to eat, to breathe, and to live. Every single food we eat on Earth starts with plants. Even the soil we use to grow plants is held together by plant roots and fertilized with the nutrients of plants that have died and **decomposed**. People have also discovered many plants that can improve health and help heal wounds and illnesses.

The roots of some trees add nutrients to the soil, which naturally fertilizes surrounding plants.

Medicinal Plants

Have you ever used green, gooey aloe vera to cool and soothe a sunburn? Aloe is a desert plant with thick leaves containing cooling goo. Aspirin comes from the willow bark tree and helps reduces swelling and pain in the body. These are just two of thousands of seeds, leaves, stems, and flowers that have healing properties. Sometimes, as with aloe, you can use the plant directly. Most of the time, people must process or prepare the plant parts to make them suitable for human use. In nearly every culture in the world, a word exists for "medicine man" or "medicine woman" to describe people knowledgeable about these plants and their uses.

aloe plant

Shade, Shelter, and Safety

From wood and tree logs to palm leaves and bamboo stalks, plants have always provided humans with shelter. By burning wood, plants also provide warmth and cooking materials for our food. Even outside, trees provide shade to avoid the sun's heat or a light shower.

Like people, most animals find safety and shelter under, inside, or on plants too. Birds build their nests in trees out of plant materials, and insects burrow into flowers and tree bark. Monkeys swing from trees, and tigers hide in tall grass to hunt.

The Uros people live on more than three dozen floating islands on Lake Titicaca, located on the border of Peru and Bolivia. The Uros use totora reeds to make their homes, boats, food, and even the islands themselves.

cocoa pods

tea plantation

Yummy Plants

Our favorite treats come from plants too. Sugar comes from sugarcane, chocolate comes from the cocoa plant, and all fruits come from plants. The sap of maple trees becomes the delicious maple syrup on pancakes. Mint comes from mint leaves, and cinnamon comes from the bark of a cinnamon tree. Coffee is water filtered through ground-up coffee beans grown throughout the world, and tea comes from soaking different flavorful plant leaves in water.

Clothing, Products, and Well-Being

Plants offer people more than food, shade, and shelter. Most clothing comes from plants as well. Cotton fibers grow out of the seed of a cotton plant after the flower bloom wilts and drops off. Linen comes from the fibers of the flax plant, and bamboo can be ground into a fiber that can be spun into yarn.

cotton plants

flax plants

bamboo plants

Plants can also make people happier and more comfortable in their environment. Think of the trees planted along roads, and public parks with carefully arranged shrubs and bushes. People beautify their yards with different types of trees, bushes, shrubs, and flowers, and they might keep houseplants, cactus, or potted trees inside. They find joy in tending gardens and decorating their homes or themselves with flowers. People also use flowers to communicate with one another, such as sending flowers to someone you love or to someone who has experienced sorrow. We commemorate people who have died with flowers, and we use them at joyous celebrations like weddings. In many cultures, different flowers carry deeply important symbolic meanings.

The Language of Flowers

In just about every culture of the world, specific flowers have symbolic meanings. In the U.S., for example, a red rose commonly represents love. The particular meanings of flowers were so important in the age of England's reign of Queen Victoria that people published books to explain what flowers meant what.

Even before then, though, flowers carried special significance. In the play *Hamlet* by William Shakespeare, one of the main characters, Ophelia, says that rosemary is "for remembrance" and that pansies represent "thoughts." Today, the flower most associated with remembrance is probably the red poppy flower. Every year on Remembrance Day, Europeans wear red poppies to honor those who died during World War I and other wars.

Leis are the garlands of flowers that Hawaiians use to beautify themselves, a custom introduced by the Polynesians when they arrived on the islands.

Oxygen

Perhaps most importantly, people and other animals need plants to release oxygen so that we can breathe. All the ways we rely on plants show why it is so important that we take care of them and give them places to grow. Over the past century or two, destruction of large forest areas, especially in the rainforest, have destroyed ecosystems and increased the amount of carbon dioxide in the atmosphere. Carbon dioxide is one of the gases in our atmosphere that traps heat and increases global temperatures. When people clear forestland for building or farming, they have to consider whether what they gain is worth what is lost.

Grow Your Own Herbs

Just about every spice in your kitchen cabinet comes from plants, primarily herbs. Even pepper is a plant, though it requires moist, humid conditions that don't exist in most of the U.S. But you can grow many popular herbs in your own kitchen.

The materials you'll need are the herbs or their seeds, a small pot or plastic container to grow them in, and water to regularly water them. You can visit a local nursery to pick out seeds or herbs already growing. Or, ask adults you know if they already are growing herbs and will give you a root to grow yourself. Sometimes herbs even grow in the wild, so you could call a local herbalist or horticulturist at a nursery or local university to find out what grows in your area.

Below are some herbs you may recognize. Others to consider include flat leaf (Italian) parsley, dill, fennel, mint, sage, thyme, rosemary, and tarragon.

Basil — used in many Italian dishes, including pizza
Oregano — a strong tasting herb also added to pizza
Cilantro/Coriander — commonly used in Mexican food and different Asian foods
Chives — add these oniony herbs to salads or meat dishes
Parsley — add to salads or garnish most dishes

Follow the instructions from the nursery or herbalist to help the plants thrive. Once your plant has grown large enough to pick the leaves, you can search online simple recipes you can make with an adult to try out different fresh herbs.

oregano

Glossary

chlorophyl (KLOR-uh-fil): the green substance in plants that uses light to manufacture food from carbon dioxide and water

decomposed (dee-kuhm-POZED): rotted or decayed

ecosystem (EE-koh-sis-tuhm): all the living things in a place and their relation to their environment

fertilization (fur-tuh-li-ZAY-shuhn): to begin reproduction in an animal or a plant by causing a sperm cell to join with an egg cell or pollen to come into contact with the reproductive part of the animal or plant

iron (EYE-urn): a strong, hard metal that is magnetic and that is used to make a great variety of things. It is also found in some foods as well as in the body's red blood cells.

molecules (MAH-luh-kyools): the smallest units that a chemical compound can be divided into that still displays all of its chemical properties. A molecule is made up of more than one atom.

nitrogen (NYE-truh-juhn): a colorless, odorless gas that makes up about four-fifths of the Earth's atmosphere

osmosis (ahz-MOH-sis or ahs-MOH-sis): the process in which a more concentrated solution passes through a membrane into a less concentrated one, until the concentrations on both sides are equal

phosphorus (FAHS-fur-uhs): a chemical element that glows in the dark. It is used in making matches, fertilizers, glass, and steel.

photosynthesis (foh-toh-SIN-thi-sis): a chemical process by which green plants and some other organisms make their food

pollinate (PAH-luh-nate): to move pollen from the stamen to the pistil of the same flower or another flower where female cells can be fertilized

predators (PRED-uh-turs): animals that live by hunting other animals for food

respiration (res-puh-RAY-shuhn): the act or process of breathing in and breathing out

starch (stahrch): a tasteless, odorless white substance found in potatoes, rice, corn, wheat, and other plant foods that is considered an important part of the human diet

Index

carbon dioxide   12, 13, 14

chlorophyll   10, 12, 16

consumer(s)   8, 37

decomposer(s)   9, 37

fertilization   24, 27

food web   37

glucose   12, 13, 14, 15

iron   35

leaves   19, 20, 23, 36

life processes   5

nitrogen   32, 34, 36

nutrients   9

organelle(s)   16, 17, 18, 19

osmosis   20, 21

oxygen   12, 13, 14, 32, 44

phosphorus   35, 36

photosynthesis   10, 12, 14, 19, 32

plant reproduction   24, 25

pollination   26, 27

producer(s)   8

roots   20

seed dispersal   28, 29, 30

starch   15

water   12, 14, 33

Show What You Know

1. How do plants produce their own food?
2. Describe how two different substances on Earth go through cycles.
3. How are animals important to plant reproduction?
4. How are plants important to the lives of people?
5. Describe what a food web is.

Websites to Visit

www.eoearth.org

www.kidsgardening.org

www.thewaterpage.com/water-conservation-kids.htm

About the Author

Tara Haelle spent much of her youth exploring creeks and forests outside and reading books inside. Her adventures became bigger when she became an adult and began traveling across the world to go on exciting adventures such as swimming with sharks, climbing Mt. Kilimanjaro, and exploring the Amazon. She earned a photojournalism degree from the University of Texas at Austin so she could keep learning about the world by interviewing scientists and writing about their work. She currently lives in central Illinois with her husband and two sons. You can learn more about her at her website: www.tarahaelle.net.

Meet The Author!
www.meetREMauthors.com

PHOTO CREDITS: Cover: leaves © Zadorozhnyi Viktor, graphic © winui; page 4 © muzzy; page 5 © kunanon; page 6-7 © Juergen Faelchle; page 7 © Pat_Hastings; page 8-9 © LSkywalker, page 9 © Alan Rockefeller, Wikipedia; page 10-11 © ArTDi101; page 11 Venus flytrap © Kuttelvaserova Stuchelova, pitcher plants © Egon Zitter, chloroplast image © Kristian Peters -- Fabelfroh; page 12 molecules © honglouwawa, glucose molecule © lyricsaima; page 13 photosynthesis © Designua, page 14 © Dr. Morley Read; page 15 © Edward Westmacott; page 16 © Designua; page 17 fresh flowers © jannoon028. dying flowers © akiyoko; page 18 © PERLA BERANT WILDER, page 19 © SNEHIT; page 20 © Dreamy Girl, page 21 cactus close-up © Patrick Poendl, activity graphic (on all pages) © siridhata, cactus night scene © Anton Foltin; page 23-24 tree rings © Sergieiev, page 24 plant © Teguh Mujiono, leaf close-up © komkrit Preechachanwate; page 25 flower diagram © Designua, inset photo full plant © Duncan Andison, flower inset photo © Stan Shebs; page 26-27 pine tree © Brian Maudsley, single bee © pixel, bee on flower © Tsekhmister; page 28-29 © Creative Travel Projects, page 29 © AlessandroZocc, page 30 © Sue Robinson, inset photo © suphanat, page 31 © Iurii Kachkovskyi; page 32-33 © Somchai Som, page 33 fallow field Israel Hervas Bengochea, water cycle © Merkushev Vasiliy, page 35 top © Kletr, center © Sebastian Kaulitzki, bottom © paul prescott; page 36 from top © A13ean, Brassica oleracea, Karduelis, Grandpa, page 37 © © Jakub Pavlinec, Paul Aniszewski, imagestalk, rck_953, Steve Byland, Volha Ahranovich, Titanchik, Jakub Pavlinec, yuris, GRASS, chantal de bruijne, Kokhanchikov, Fedorov Oleksiy; page 38 © Deyan Georgiev, page 39 plant © Vitaly Raduntsev, inset © Smit; page 40-41 © Michal Knitl, page 41 top © Valentyn Volkov, bottom © Nickolai Repnitskii; page 42 top © THPStock, middle © Elena Elisseeva, bottom © 06photo, page 43 © Deborah Kolb; page 44-45 © Rich Carey, page 45 © Gts

Edited by: Keli Sipperley

Cover and Interior design by: Nicola Stratford   www.nicolastratford.com

Library of Congress PCN Data

Edible Sunlight / Tara Haelle
(Let's Explore Science)
ISBN 978-1-68191-399-5 (hard cover)
ISBN 978-1-68191-441-1 (soft cover)
ISBN 978-1-68191-480-0 (e-Book)
Library of Congress Control Number: 2015951566

Also Available as:

ROURKE'S
e-Books